FOREX
STRATEGIES

FOREX STRATEGIES

 FOREX STRATEGIES

INDEX

What is Forex Trading?

Importance of Forex Trading

Four main types of orders in the Forex market

Price Movements of Forex Trading: How and Why Markets Move and How to Make Profits

- You predict Forex spending trends
- Market obeys Scientific Laws
- Business can be made from the news
- Current expenditure trends
- Win the contest
- Be imperfect but never a loser

Forex Traders: The Need to Be Objective

- Forex Trading Tools
- The strategy of the three trend lines

How To Win With Forex: Secrets Step By Step

- Success comes from within
- Discipline and Losses

FOREX STRATEGIES

- A commercial advantage
- Success is in your hands

The Dangers of Getting Emotional About Forex Trading

Forex Trading Strategy - Channel Breakdown

Forex Killer vs. Forex

Power Strategy

The Right Time in Forex Trading

- Proper use of support and strength
- Why buying low and selling high doesn't work
- You have to have guts, but you make money.

The Importance of Real-Time Forex Charts

Calculation of interest on

Forex Trading

Advantages of Automated Forex Trading

Choosing the Right Automated Forex Trading Software

 FOREX STRATEGIES

What is Forex Trading?

Forex trading involves trading international currencies. Here you can sell the currency of one country to buy the currency of another. The trader trades in [Forex] currencies at the most appropriate time to profit from the transaction. A good forecasting ability plays a key role in this regard. One may wonder how Forex trading can be such a lucrative profit opportunity since the fluctuations in the exchange are so small.

But remember, when done in large volumes, a minor change can mean a lot. It also has many non-monetary advantages. Anyone who wants to trade on Forex can do so, as only basic knowledge is required.

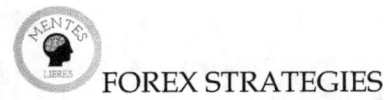 FOREX STRATEGIES

Forex can help you make a lot of money. But there are certain conditions to follow before trading Forex. First of all, you need to have a thorough knowledge of stock market trends, the fundamentals of trading and the ability to take risks. You will get all the help you need to reach these conditions very easily.

There are many sites on the Internet that can help you clarify your fundamentals and help you cope with bad weather. One good reason why Forex trading can be considered is the fact that there are frequent fluctuations in currencies, although in percentage terms it can be small.

You win if the fluctuation favors you and the opposite is also true. No one can accurately predict the trend of currencies. Liquidity is another reason why Forex trading is so popular.

Now the most important part - in Forex, you can make large sums of money even if your initial investment is on a lower side. You can invest as little as $50,000. Rich people do not have a maximum limit for the amount of investment. So remember that even with a nominal investment, the earning capacity is certainly very large.

Most large companies are connected to the Internet world today, and Forex trading is no exception. You can trade foreign exchange from home. In fact, it is done entirely online. You have the freedom to choose when you want to trade, and you don't need to meet any deadlines.

Basically, you can be your own boss. The online trading process is simple enough for anyone to understand. You just need to open an account to trade Forex with a recognized broker and they will complete the rest of the formalities. All you have to do is prepare with the amount of your investment.

Therefore, it is clear that Forex trading can be one of the best deals to make money. Although there is a level of risk associated with it, but it can be avoided with due care and an alert mind!

Importance of Forex Trading

Foreign exchange [Forex] involves the exchange of different foreign currencies to make a profit. The reason for buying the currency of another country may be the need to buy some merchandise from that country as well, in addition to earning money through the difference in exchange rates.

In the latter case, people buy currency from a foreign country when the rate in the market is low, and sell it when the rates go up. Foreign exchange trading is normally conducted between central banks, the government, speculators and multinational

 FOREX STRATEGIES

corporations. Nations cannot trade with each other without the presence of a foreign market.

A large amount of money is traded daily on the Forex market, although the amount invested by an individual trader can be very low. No one individually can influence Forex fluctuations, not even the government. Therefore, one can easily conclude that the currency level reflects the strength or weakness of a country's economy. This makes the Forex market a good place for competition.

The government and central bank try to stabilize your country's currency by speculating, buying and selling currencies at the right times. However, they can influence the market if they trade in large volumes. To

buy their own currency, however, the government or central bank must have huge foreign exchange reserves with them. Therefore, it is practically impossible to artificially inflate the value of the currency.

Banks trade a lot in foreign exchange and this is a part of the volume in the Forex market. They buy currencies not only as individual entities, but also on behalf of their clients. They trade many futures. Until a few years ago, brokers were able to influence trading volumes on the Forex market. But due to the electronic services available today, broker services are not necessary. It is easy to trade electronically.

Trading with international countries is only possible with the existence of Forex markets. When there is no Forex market, there is no common currency between two countries, so one cannot evaluate the value of one currency against the other.

The buyer pays the seller in the seller's currency. With the money thus received, the seller buys goods in the buyer's country and sells those goods in his [seller's] country.

Only then can he know how much he has earned from the export. However, in the presence of a Forex market, it is very easy for a seller to know his profits the instant he makes an export transaction. Similarly, the buyer will also have a deep knowledge of the cost he will have to incur to buy goods from an international country.

Four main types of orders in the Forex market

There are many types of orders that traders can place to make transactions in the Forex market, in order to profit from them.

- **Market Order**

The market order is the simplest and most common. In this case, the trader buys and sells the currency at the exchange rate prevailing in the market at the time the order is placed. Due to the large size of the market and the high volatility, trends can be reversed at any time, so people prefer to

FOREX STRATEGIES

place orders at the market price to protect themselves from any adverse trend.

- **Restraining order**

In this case, the trader specifies a price at which he may want to buy or sell the currency. Suppose a trader has bought GBP against the USD at 1.9710, then he can place a sell order at 1.9725, when the exchange executes the order and he benefits from it. The order will be cancelled if the target price is not reached during the day.

- **Stop Loss Order**

Due to volatility, stop losses are essential. They determine the maximum loss a trader is willing to suffer. Suppose that in the above case, the risk capacity of the trader is low, then he can place a stop loss at 1.9705, at which level the change will register losses for him, and he will not be affected by any fall below 1.9705.

- **Entry order**

This order is only executed when certain conditions are met in the market, which the order specifies. The entry order can be a limit entry order or even a stop entry order.

- **Entry Order of Limits**

For example, suppose the current market price for GBP/USD is 1.9705-10. This implies that the trader can trade at these levels. Here, a trader can place an entry limit order to sell his shares at a price above the market price, say, 1.9715. Your order would only be executed if that price is reached. In the same way, you can place a buy order at a level of, say, 1.9700, and your "buy" order will remain pending until the price falls to that level.

- **Entry stop order**

This order is generally used when the trader has reason to believe that the currency is trading in a fixed range and believes he is on the verge of a breach of that range. You may want to buy at a price higher than the market price or sell at a price lower than the market price. In the same example, the trader can go ahead and buy at 1.9720 or sell at 1.9690, where he believes that once these levels are reached, the currency will only rise or fall further, as the case may be. A trader exerts a stop entry order only when he has reasonable grounds to believe that there will be sharp movements in exchange rates in the Forex market.

FOREX STRATEGIES

Price Movements of Forex Trading: How and Why Markets Move and How to Make Profits

Understanding Forex spending trends is not easy. Businessmen often have misconceptions and make agendas based on them and suffer losses. The following can help you understand trends:

You predict Forex spending trends

Businessmen look at a certain level and jump to it thinking it's stable. However, this is simply based on assumptions and that never works in the Forex business. There is no accurate prediction.

If the goal is to win, you have to base the business on trends of safe shooting expenses. In connection with this, there are certain factors that are listed below.

Market obeys Scientific Laws

There is a notion that market trends are

based on logic. Some believers are Gann, Elliot and the followers of Fibonacci.

However, if everyone knew everything, prices would never have been a surprise and markets would be non-existent. The profane would accept these ideas and their fantastic suggestions. However, the facts say otherwise.

Business can be made from the news

It is not advisable, as the news is insignificant. The way news is supposed to decide movements. Let's see how trends happen.

FOREX STRATEGIES

Current expenditure trends

Basic concepts + Individual vision of the same = Trends of the Forex market

People are rarely rational. They often function emotionally, so logical reasoning is not always true. True human psychology is consistent, but these issues have no logic:

1. People make costs move to the extreme and these waypoints can be used profitably.

2. Go on with the business. Don't get into riddles.

 FOREX STRATEGIES

Win the contest

Forex is a sport and competition is based on opportunities. You may not be able to determine the possibilities, but you will never lose.

This does not apply to all cases, but try it in situations of high probability and you will surely get the cake with very few losses. Make big profits in good time.

Voracity and panic fluctuate costs, creating points that are visible in Forex programs and can be used profitably.

 FOREX STRATEGIES

It's a game so that when prices fluctuate on your side, you get to work. Control your finances well and be a winner.

Be imperfect but never a loser

Forex markets are full of those who try to guess and try to get an undisclosed non-existent trend figure. Although Forex spending trends seem messy, basing your business on cost fluctuations will make you a winner.

It may not be an ideal business for many; however, if done well, you can make a lot of money through forex trading.

Forex Traders: The Need to Be Objective

It is difficult for Forex traders to realize that the currency market is extremely unpredictable. As new traders spend a lot of time trying to learn the mechanics of forex trading and focus their time and energy on trying to find a method to predict movements, they naturally expect there to be rules governing market movement. This is not the case; many traders are at a disadvantage.

While Forex traders have a number of tools at their disposal that allow them to judge the right time to open or close a position, many prefer to rely on a single tool. So, when opening a position, they look at their favorite indicator and, to a large extent, base their trading decisions solely on it, ignoring others.

This works well enough until that indicator starts telling them something different from what others are. Traders trapped in an open position that their favorite tool tells them to hold will often do so, despite the fact that other tools are telling them to close and exit the market, and end up losing money.

The basic problem, of course, is that the trader is not looking at the market as it is, but through the lens of his own expectations of it and also using his favorite indicator to reinforce those ideas rather than looking at the big picture. And, encouraged by the fact that the indicator chosen is the profit forecast

you want, the trader is focusing more on money than on the market.

If the Forex market were not unpredictable, it would collapse because all traders would benefit all the time. There are many tools that can help traders predict the direction of the market and usually do an efficient job. But even in the hands of the most experienced traders, the best tools sometimes fail to correctly predict market movements.

Losing in trading due to erroneous market prediction is an innate part of Forex trading and traders need to accept it. In addition, they need to learn to avoid being in a position where they don't have many options.

To do this, the trader needs to accept the fact that the forex market has a mind of its own and traders have to follow their moves rather than trying to make it go in the direction they want.

Forex Trading Tools

There is no single super smart forex trading tool that gives you profit, profit and more profit. The only possible solution is to use a combination of different tools to identify favorable market forces and obtain a maximum number of high probability trades over a period of time. Trend lines are the most popular and reliable Forex trading tool that many successful traders testify to.

The strategy of the three trend lines

Trend lines are an important tool for identifying and confirming trends in technical analysis. It is a straight line that connects two or more price points and then extends into the future to guide you.

There will be lines drawn through significant lows in an uptrend, and significant highs in a downtrend.

To more or less classify trend lines, we can divide them into three: short term trend lines, medium term trend lines and long term trend lines.

 FOREX STRATEGIES

1. **Short-term trend lines**

Draw these lines through the two most recent lows for an uptrend or through the two most recent highs for a downtrend. The best observations are found in a shorter time frame, such as a 15-minute or 30-minute chart.

2. **Medium-term trend lines**

These are best observed in a higher time frame, as in a 60-minute chart. It connects the closest price action to the closest significant price action to the current price action with the previous significant price action in an uptrend or the closest significant price action to the current price action with the previous significant price action in a downtrend.

3. Long-term trend lines

Use higher time frames such as the 4-hour chart or daily chart to draw long-term trend lines using the same method as medium-term trend lines. The long term trend line is considered an effective tool for Forex trading. The daily chart is mainly used by traders of large institutions that do not usually make small movements at intraday level.

By drawing a trend line on a daily chart you can graphically analyze where the price is and where it is likely to rebound. But use trend lines as a tool to trade Forex with caution and discretion. Covering your charts with all possible trend lines will result in confusion and blurred analysis.

It is not a good idea to rely completely on a short-term trendline. They simply give you a definite picture of the current price action. These are often broken during the course of a day. Their main use is to provide you with a clear and instantly recognizable graphical representation of current price behavior.

If you notice that the price re-tests a trend line in the higher time frames, look at other factors. Draw horizontal lines to mark key support and resistance using the above ups and downs. Draw retracement and extension levels of Fibonacci. Calculate the daily pivot points and put them on your chart. Have the 200 EMA (Exponential Moving Average) shown on your charts.

 FOREX STRATEGIES

How To Win With Forex: Secrets Step By Step

When 95% of traders lose money, what makes you think you can win? To see your chances of success as a Forex trader, here is a checklist for you to see and become one of the elite traders, who make huge long-term profits.

The following are some ways to lose money. You may want to change your mind immediately if you are thinking of trying one of them. Do this to avoid losses and continue your Forex education!

FOREX STRATEGIES

1. Following a Forex Robot with Simulated Profits - You can apparently achieve success without any effort as promised by them. You are asked to accept your simulated tracking records backwards. Your capital will be destroyed when you try them.

2. Day Trading and Scalping - Due to short-term random volatility, it simply doesn't work. Like robots, even the people who sell them always have a simulated history.

Many more of these fall into the category of trying to find someone else to give you success. This doesn't work in currency markets.

Aside from needing a commercial advantage, you also need to understand the ways and reasons that lead to success. Let's look at this in detail.

Success comes from within

The combination of a simple and robust help to understand and operate with discipline is what forex trading is all about.

You need to know what you are doing to trade with discipline. This translates into having confidence, which you definitely don't get from someone who tells you what to do. You gain confidence through your own knowledge and learning.

 FOREX STRATEGIES

Discipline and Losses

As you have to keep executing trading signals through lost periods, discipline is difficult. This has to continue until you hit a home run, even when the market cheats you and takes your money.

A commercial advantage

What separates your forex trading system from the 95% losers is your trading advantage. You can answer what your trading advantage is and how it will help you beat the majority. You don't have one if you don't know what it is.

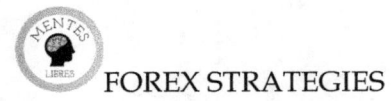 FOREX STRATEGIES

Few succeed in simply searching for foreign exchange trading. These elements are present in the trading strategy of the winners:

Using a simple and robust forex trading system

- Have a solid foundation in the fundamentals of forex trading

- Know exactly why your system will lead to success

- Have the confidence and discipline to follow through with your plan

- Knowing that they alone are responsible for

your success in Forex trading

You have to be alone, have confidence in your actions and be disciplined to follow your plan in foreign exchange trading.

Success is in your hands

It sounds simple, however, it actually depends on your approach to foreign exchange trading - with the right mindset and getting the right education. The trader outperforms himself, rather than the market beating the trader in forex trading.

Learn the basics, get the right system, have confidence, get an advantage and be

disciplined. Do all this to enjoy the success of forex trading.

 FOREX STRATEGIES

The Dangers of Getting Emotional About Forex Trading

Getting excited in the stock market is the worst thing that can happen to investors. The same goes for Forex traders. Seeing paper losses in daily trading is quite common.

Once you make the decision to buy something and make losses, you still cling even though situations turn from bad to worse, just because you feel that things could turn in your favor once again. The main problem here is that, the decision to stay in a losing trade for a long time is emotional, as you are not in the mood to accept a loss and get out of the trade.

The Forex market is largely influenced by the general market and you should always trade based on market-based indications, and not just start one as your heart tells you to do so. Sometimes, you may be so emotionally attached to a given currency in the Forex market that most of your exposure to the Forex market would be in that particular currency.

There is nothing wrong with it, as if you had reasonable grounds to believe that the currency will do well, then you will really benefit from the change. The 'wrong' thing is to open a trade in a currency just because your heart tells you to.

 FOREX STRATEGIES

In the case, if you feel strongly about any currency, then it is best to check the reality by taking into account what the market is indicating. This will give you a clear idea of whether or not you should trade in that currency.

The basic thing to remember is that once you have started a trade, and you are incurring paper losses, and by all indications, things are likely to get even worse for you, then it is much better to account for the losses and get out of it rather than stick to it until the moment when ultimately you are able to see some gains from it. Remember, markets have little room for emotions.

Forex trading is not a win-win situation. Be prepared to lose on some trades as well. That's the precise way the market works. It's not really a question of whether you're right or not, the fact is that markets move in an unexpected way and have the ability to surprise people when they least expect it. All the fundamentals and even experience can be thrown into the air when the markets decide to do something.

So follow the directions the market gives you. If you feel that after starting a trade, things are not going the way you expected, reserve your losses and get out of it. You can invest the amount in some other trade and make good profits instead of keeping your lost trade.

 FOREX STRATEGIES

Forex Trading Strategy - Channel Breakdown

The Forex system is the world's largest trade. It takes advantage of some movements so that businessmen earn well. An accepted Forex business agenda that is used quite profitably in the business is called Channel Breakout.

Forex Trading Channels - Channels consist of routes made on a schedule to track the matrix where the exchange had been made in a period of time. They can be constructed in a simple way. Observe the schedule in a time lapse and draw lines that link comparatively high spot business expenses, and down in the

FOREX STRATEGIES

linkage of comparatively low spot business expenses. This will give you an image of the existing business matrix over a time period of about six months.

Channel Breakout - Once the exchange value goes up the peak network line, there is a growing network leak. In addition, once the value drops below the lowest point of the network, you get a leak down the network. Network leaks occur up and down. With enough Forex information with scientific scrutiny, everyone can use the process to get a paid exchange business agenda.

Channels have to be built very carefully. Every line meeting does not indicate a proper exit. If there is any fallacy in the construction of the line, what is observed are the businesses outside the matrix, which simply takes you back inside. So, first of all, get enough Forex knowledge.

Gained Control of Forex Channels - When you discover how networks work, profits will occur. Build the business with enough pauses. Then, in case of an incorrect escape signal, you will get tolerable losses or if luck favors you, a very low profit.

But if you are on the right side of a proper network leak, the small fault you received will be removed and you will get a good and satisfactory profit.

Any worthwhile Forex business shareholder capitalizes channel leaks. In case you want to cash in on the foreign exchange markets, devote a certain amount of time to Forex

education to build this agenda and various processes of technological scrutiny.

This will strengthen the trading agendas, which will have beneficial consequences. If you don't have time to fully understand the bets and yields contained in a Forex business agenda, you may not get the desired consequences. As you can see, your profit is up to you.

Forex Killer vs. Forex Power Strategy

For those who have an interest in the huge currency market of 3 trillion dollars a day, it is common knowledge that in order to stay on the right side of the Forex market what you need is to constantly discover new plans to minimize your losses and maximize your profits, and always adapt so that you can take advantage of any and every opportunity to get a greater share in the pie.

The Forex Assassin formula and the Forex Power Strategy course are two of the most widely used currency trading tools. These two tools have been heavily criticized, but their operating principles are completely different. As a Forex trader, how would you understand which tool is best for you? To help you out of your confusion, read on.

The Forex Assassin formula is designed as a solution to the problems of the busy man with forex trading. This tool is ideal for an average of 9 to 5 professionals who wish to generate additional income through Forex trading, but cannot gather the time to monitor markets throughout the day or study complex technical formulas, analysis and charts.

Forex Assassin is a simple and convenient strategy that can be used with little or no understanding of how the market actually works. It usually takes about a quarter of an hour each week to prepare and assign a

trading strategy, after which you just have to relax and let the market do its job.

It is very simple, but on the other hand it is also quite limited, as it does not require much knowledge of the market. The goal is to allow the mannequin to earn limited money by minimizing his chances of loss, which, however, is not the best way to earn the most money.

On the contrary, the Forex Power Strategy tool offers a detailed and in-depth course on the dynamics and economy of the market. It takes into account a large amount of material, and includes all levels of trading. As a result, a large investment of time and attention is required to make the most of the course and absorb its lessons. So, unless you can devote enough time to it, the Forex Energy Strategy tool is not for you.

But in return, you have the assurance that by the time you finish the course, you will have achieved a better and more solid knowledge of how the market works and, therefore, your profit potential will be correspondingly greater.

But no matter which tool you choose, using either tool is better than trading blindly in the market and ending up with big losses.

The Right Time in Forex Trading

When you perceive a business opportunity, the deciding factor is knowing exactly when to buy. Unfortunately, this is the point at which most people lose the argument by inadequately timing their entry levels. But here are some basic guidelines to help you in those crucial moments:

Proper use of support and strength

If you try to use the fundamental rule of the stock market - "buy low, sell high" - in Forex trading, you will actually lose money. To understand it is necessary to know how the support and resistance system works.

A support price is a historically proven price at which traders intervene and buy in order to "support the market". The more times this price is tested, the more bankable the support price will be.

Conversely, a resistance level is defined as a level at which "prices resisted rising". Also in this case, the more times this level is tested, the more reliable it will be.

FOREX STRATEGIES

Why buying low and selling high doesn't work

The reason this traditional wisdom is counterproductive in Forex trading is that if you really wait for prices to drop, you will end up missing out on some of the best opportunities to make money. Consider: when a currency starts to recover, what are the chances of it withdrawing?

What if it doesn't and stabilizes? If you are still waiting for a withdrawal, you could end up never entering the trade because most currency changes occur from new market highs and without any kind of withdrawal.

 FOREX STRATEGIES

So, if you plan to focus your Forex trading strategy on waiting for a supportive price entry, wake up! You can lose in the most profitable trades. What your Forex trading strategy should aim at is rather "buy high and sell higher", i.e. you should try to do just the opposite of what people in general are doing. Try to keep an eye out for any advances in support and resistance, and then sell and buy accordingly.

You have to have guts, but you make money.

The policy of going against the crowd requires courage to practice. But think strategy with a cool head and you'll see that's the most logical thing you can do. How many times have you heard of traders buying support, but the market.

And once again, haven't you heard that the price keeps rising and never reaches the support, which makes the trader miss the opportunity to take advantage of the trend?

So instead of being traditional and losing money, it's easier to adopt the breakthrough policy: you won't feel comfortable coming in, but you will make money. The trick is to break with the pattern established by the losing majority and do what is productive and logical considering the common and predictable answer.

FOREX STRATEGIES

The Importance of Real-Time Forex Charts

Do you want to make money in the foreign exchange market? To achieve this, you must possess a deep technical knowledge, focused on the ability to track currency exchange rates, through the interpretation of real forex charts.

If you are an amateur in this field, you should quickly discover authentic Internet Forex charts or you can opt for free real Forex charts. The best option is, however, to take the help of free card recognition software and master it, you are well prepared for this business.

 FOREX STRATEGIES

Online forex charts keep you up to date on currency values at any time, even between short periods of time, such as minutes, and long intervals, such as several years. Charts that represent rate swings are line charts, or bar charts or candlestick charts.

Line charts are easy to interpret and help you comprehensively review price highs and lows. It helps you follow the current trend of the exchange rate movement. In contrast, bar charts are not as lucid as line charts, but provide very detailed information.

To summarize, the length of a bar chart represents the amount of price rise or fall and the amplitude gives the duration, which has witnessed this. The initial and final rates are mentioned on the chart so that you can identify the range and whether it is a fall or a rise. There is pattern recognition software available that interprets the bar charts for you and makes your task easier.

The Japanese were the first to use candlestick charts to plot the amount of their rice production. Since then they have become increasingly popular. Although they are similar to bar charts, they are colored.

Each color acts as a code to signify the price rise or fall. The index is written on the graph itself. Therefore, candlestick charts are much easier to use than bars. Candlestick charts have unique patterns and are so pretty as to be so called by natural beauties. As soon as you can identify the particular pattern, you will identify the market trend.

A real currency chart is often complemented by many technical indicators such as trend, strength, volatility and cyclical movements. A forex chart is useful in itself, but this attached information is provided to facilitate your task of market analysis to predict both market movements and market volume.

 FOREX STRATEGIES

Calculation of interest on Forex Trading

One of the best things about Forex trading is the fact that one can trade using leverage; therefore borrow up to 1,000 times your capital in order to make a trade. However, borrowing money to trade in foreign currencies is the same as borrowing it for other purposes: interest must be paid on the loan.

However, since currency trading involves both buying and selling, the interest due on your loan can be offset by the interest earned on the currency you buy. Before turning to concrete examples, let's take a look at interest rates in general, to see how it affects the forex market.

In central banks, interest rates are set according to a country's monetary policy: high interest rates make the currency more expensive to buy and low interest rates make it less expensive.

Imagine that the government of a country with high inflation will help you understand how interest rates are used.

The government, due to rapidly rising prices, may decide to raise interest rates. This would increase the cost of the country's currency and bring down demand and consumption, as loans would be more expensive.

 FOREX STRATEGIES

This, in turn, would cause prices and inflation rates to fall. Similarly, a country in recession could lower interest rates to boost the country's economy, as a lower currency price would lead to increased demand and, therefore, supply.

Interest rates set by central banks also determine the rate at which commercial banks can borrow from governments and lend to their customers, including foreign exchange traders. This tells us how interest rates affect this trade.

A trader, who, for example, buys GBP/USD, needs to borrow the dollars to buy the pounds and will therefore pay interest on the USD and earn it with the GBP. If the interest rate the Bank of England sets for the pound sterling is higher than that set by the Federal Reserve for the US dollar, the trader will earn more on the pounds sterling he bought than on the US dollars he borrowed, thus making a profit.

However, unless there is a significant difference between the two interest rates, the net result will be marginal. In addition, while interest rates are fixed on an annual basis, trading positions are generally opened for short periods. This serves to significantly reduce any gain or loss on interest rates.

Advantages of Automated Forex Trading

Currency trading is today the preferred form of investment for a growing number of people these days. It is clear why this is so.

As the world's largest trading market, the Forex market has a steadily growing trading volume, which has increased from about $500 billion to about $2 trillion over the past twenty years.

In addition, since it is not tied to any particular trading floor, this is an unusually liquid market. Trading 24 hours a day also makes it a permanently open market. Therefore, since many markets open and close at the same time, markets around the world can be effectively tracked.

Therefore, both large and small traders are attracted to Forex trading. They enjoy a wide range of trading strategies based on the various aspects of exchange rates. Many traders who enter the market find the different things that affect currency exchange rates very attractive for a very simple reason: they can use a wide range of tools when working in this exciting and stimulating market.

Automation is perhaps the biggest influence today on the future growth of the Forex market, as it brings more advantages than disadvantages. Manual systems attempting to trade in a volatile and fast-paced environment bring with them a number of losses.

A simple delay in buying and selling can cause a row of losses in a manual system and thus cause the trader immense frustration. Automated Forex trading allows trading to take place anywhere in the world, in real time, and eliminates losses seen in manual systems.

Trading in a wide range of different currency markets at the same time, without worrying about the time zones of the locations in question, is another advantage of automated Forex trading. Sitting in New York at 2 a.m., you can do business with traders from different countries on the other side of the world simultaneously and with great ease.

All thanks to automated Forex trading.

Risk management is often a source of concern for traders, but even this is reduced with automated Forex trading. Payments can now be synchronized in real time and this leaves traders satisfied, unlike manual trades, where there is always uncertainty about the payment that is made after the completion of the trade. The automated trading system is progressively being developed, which brings with it the hope that the settlement system will be updated and the market risks will soon disappear.

If there is one technology that has advanced by leaps and bounds in recent years, it is information technology. In fact, it is expected to continue to grow for many years to come. More importantly, advances in computer technology are good for traders who want access to the best automated Forex trading.

Access to technology easily and cheaply from the comfort of traders' homes means that they can manage their own investments with ease. Therefore, automated forex trading will be a welcome addition to a fully trained investment vehicle for those who trade in the forex world.

 FOREX STRATEGIES

Choosing the Right Automated Forex Trading Software

Automated currency trading has its own advantages. Here all you have to do is follow the trade signals that are generated and if you are able to execute them with discipline and if your system is logical, then you can easily accumulate profits.

Before we analyze the various ways in which you can make profits through this software, let's take a look at what you shouldn't do.

Many traders find forex robots online and

buy them. But you should keep in mind that most of these are pieces of garbage and have never been traded in real time. Take a look at the history and then the disclaimer. It is probably hypothetical or stimulated and that is not a sure indication of future results. It's strange how someone can just take a test and say they make money off it.

Of course, they make money for the seller, they get the sale of the software and the trader is whipped in the market. No one gets $100,000 of annual income for $100,000. You will never make money with these stimulated systems, so try to stay away from them.

Let's take a look now at how automated currency trading is done the right way and discuss the options.

Buy a system with a history that has been audited for two years. They may not be cheap, but they can pay for themselves many times over. Just make sure you understand and agree with the logic before you start using it.

Try free systems. Browse our other articles to find out more about them and you'll realize why this is a great place to start your automated forex trading career.

Go ahead, build yours. This is easier than it looks. It's also a better way to trade because if you build and customize the system, you'll gain more confidence and be able to trade with discipline, even during periods of loss.

 FOREX STRATEGIES

If you decide to build a system yourself, we have it covered in our articles. But the best way to do this is to trade in outbreaks, new highs or lows, have momentum indicators to time your moves and focus on long-term trends. The simpler, the better. This will allow you to cope with changing market conditions. Filling it with too many indicators could spoil it.

Once you are in possession of a system, get a forex software package, program the rules and everything is ready.

Keep in mind that all forex trading systems, including the best ones, will suffer losses that can continue for a long period of time. You need to continue trading until you make a home run and because of this discipline and money management it is necessary.

 FOREX STRATEGIES

If your system makes between 50-100% compounded annually, you are part of the best automated forex trading software and can trade in the markets and enjoy the success of forex trading.

 FOREX STRATEGIES

Visit our author page on Amazon and get more MENTES LIBRES!

http://amazon.com/author/menteslibres

If you wish, you can leave a comment on this book by clicking on the following link so that we can continue to grow! Thank you very much for your purchase!

https://www.amazon.com/dp/B082B4FG8Z

www.ingramcontent.com/pod-product-compliance
Lightning Source LLC
Chambersburg PA
CBHW070815220526
45466CB00002B/673